The Soul Letters You Never Received

- A 3-part series -

Vol 3: Show Up just as You Are

Deep Roots and Soaring Wings...

Copyright 2022 © Natacha Dauphin
All Rights Reserved

The right of Natacha Dauphin to be the author of this work has been asserted in accordance with the Copyright, Designs and Patents Act 1988.

This is the first edition publishing through KDP (November 2022) and all rights remain with the author Natacha Dauphin.

No part of this publication may be reproduced, stored or transmitted in any form or by any means without prior written consent from the author.

Enquiries: honouringyourcreativefire@gmail.com

ISBN: 9798578044298

# Contents

| | |
|---|---|
| **Prologue** | **5** |
| | |
| **COURAGE** | **7** |
| Brave, Wise, and Rebellious | 9 |
| Wild, Authentic, and Perfectly Imperfect | 53 |
| | |
| **COMMITMENT AND DEVOTION** | **89** |
| Choose | 91 |
| Let Go | 127 |
| Reclaim | 141 |
| | |
| **DEDICATION AND CO-CREATION** | **161** |
| The Return of the Muse, Patience, and Perseverance | 163 |
| Soul Activation | 191 |
| Co-Creation with Source | 215 |
| | |
| **BLISS** | **239** |
| The Power of Alchemy and Transmutation | 241 |
| Surrendering to a Blissful Life | 281 |
| | |
| **Epilogue** | **313** |
| | |
| **Dedication** | **315** |
| | |
| **About The Author** | **316** |

*My books*
*Are powerhouses*
*Disguised*
*As wooden shacks.*

# Prologue

Volume III of *The Soul Letters You Never Received* marks the completion of this trilogy. May it be a trampoline for you to integrate, plant new seeds, and bounce into the arena of your life - the one beyond your imagination.

Each and every one of the pieces in this series has the potential to be a portal. Walk through the ones you feel called to walk through with an open heart and a curious mind.

My wish is that these words find you somewhere on your journey and offer you a hand, a doorway, a path, a hug, a reminder from my soul to yours to live a soul-led life.

At different times in life, you will have more or less capacity for huge external leaps. Honour your own rhythm, your own cycles. Show Up just as You Are means exactly this: Show Up JUST as YOU ARE in THIS VERY MOMENT. No mask, no pretending, no pushing, no lying. Perhaps today it means to nourish your heart, or to dare something new, or to set some boundaries. Listen. Listen, and act accordingly.

The world does not need more people who betray themselves, who discard their heart, body wisdom, soul calling, and intuition. It needs more connected people who honour life and bring to it their true unique essence. This means stepping into that arena. For it is outside the comfort zone that magic truly blossoms.

Root, rise, and shine. Reclaim your voice and the courage to use it. Show up as the powerful, perfectly imperfect, magnificent being that you are. You deserve this. Choose your life. You have the right and power to do so.

Commit to yourself and to your journey on this beautiful planet with gratitude. Bring the sacred back through ceremony, devotion, dedication, connection, creativity, play, and most of all presence. Allow the magic of love, courage, and alchemy to invite you to dance a delicious and blissful life.

May these pages hold your hand as you do just that.

# COURAGE

Brave, Wise, and Rebellious

*

Wild, Authentic, and Perfectly Imperfect

There is no time left
To hide.

All those seconds
Have been counted.

Life has found you.

Show up,
Stand up,
And shine your light.

Brave, Wise, and Rebellious

One must be courageous

To choose

To recommit

To life,

Happiness,

And inner peace,

On a daily basis.

The only way
To not miss out
Is to show up.

By this,
I do not mean
That you have to do, and do, and do.

But in order not to miss out on your life,
You must be brave,
Step into your unique power,
And do your thing.

Show up for yourself.

Commit, trust, and surrender.

It really is that simple and straightforward.

## I AM WILLING

I am willing
To see
From a different perspective.

I am willing
To embrace
Change.

I am willing
To let go
Of what no longer serves me.

I may sometimes struggle with this.

But...

I am willing.

Do apologise
For hurtful actions
And behaviour.

But don't ever
Be ashamed
Of who you are.

And don't ever
Apologise
For who you are.

I have forgotten
What I was asked to remember
Long, long ago.

And there is no way back.

I must seek again.
Find my way.
Reach out.
Reach in.

There is no way back.

There is a way here,
And a way forward.

With every step,
The web is being woven,
The threads renewed,
The wheel realigned.

The old transforms                        1/2

And reincarnates
Into new forms.
Wisdom is passed on.
Alternative insights,
And new frequencies
Embraced.

We are rewriting history
With every breath,
With every intention.

Don't be scared.
Breathe.

All is well.

The excitement
Of sticking your foot out
Of your comfort zone
And realising
That this is where
You and your foot belong,
Is pretty awesome.

This piece was written for you
While you were slaying
Your most tenacious demon.

You used to think
You were a nobody,
With a nothing
About you.

Now you know
You are a somebody,
With a sword
And a gentle but brave heart.

Ready to take on
Any needed battle,
Yet, ready to surrender
To the flow of the river.

For you ARE a somebody,
And you are ALL.

1/2

All that is,
And all that will ever be.

Do not settle
For what you think
You should be or do.

Instead, follow what ignites your fire
With awareness and gratitude.

This might take some time and wandering.

You may rise and fall.
You may not be able to settle for a while.
You may feel lost and confused,
And that's OK.

This path is one of deep integrity
And abundant blessings.

Awareness is great.

Knowing what to do
With that awareness
Is brilliance.

A frustrated creative being
Is not a pretty sight.

So do yourself, and others, a favour.

Get started.
Honour your fire.
Put in the work.

Then go and share it with the world.
This is non-negotiable.

Whether anyone pays attention or not,
Is none of your business.

The time has come
To fully embrace who you are.

Magic will happen.

Rise

Woman

Rise.

Not to start a war

Against men,

But to stop the fight

With and against yourself.

Stop shrinking.
Stop hiding.

Pull off
The masks.

Allow yourself
To be vulnerable.

Allow yourself
To be seen.

Allow yourself to be witnessed.

It is that leap of courage,
That stepping outside of what's familiar,
That will make you feel fully alive.

You are a rainbow,
Whether you know it or not.
Born from the sacred union
Of rain and sun.                    1/2

Show up
As the full,
Authentic expression
Of you.

The main thing

That helps us

Cut through

The limiting protective layers,

Is to take that step,

To give ourselves

The experience

Of freedom and expression

We so deeply crave.

Stop knocking
At the door.

Just go in.

Step into your aligned power.

Only then
Will the threat
Of external forces
Melt away.

I am taking the risk.

Because I'd rather
Take a step
Towards faith and trust
Than drown
In fear and cynicism.

Summon the courage
To initiate.

Then the courage
To patiently allow the echo.

Then the courage
To strike again,
When you hear the inner signal.

Some days

Showing up

Is finding the courage

To get out of bed

When your mind

Is playing nasty tricks on you.

Keep that sword nearby
For those days
When you inadvertently
Let those distorted thoughts in.

Then pick up the sword
And slay the delusion
Will all your heart,
With all your courage,

Reminding yourself
That you are
Far from a fraud,

That you are a warrior of light,
A co-creator of beauty and magic,
In service to life.

Do not chase the passing bee
When she believes your buds are empty.

Keep your roots strong,
Your stems growing,
And your blossoms abundant.

Trust.

Another bee WILL come.

Rebirth is a process.

It is likely to be
Painful,
Exhilarating,
And exhausting.

But what it gifts you,
Will always be
Far beyond your imagination.

Today, I feel neither strong nor weak,
Neither big nor small,
Neither happy nor sad,
But I have arrived.

I feel neither seen nor invisible,
Neither accomplished nor incompetent,
Neither proud nor ashamed,
Neither a success nor a failure,
But I have arrived.

I have arrived,
In this place of deep surrender and peace.
I have arrived,
Where everything and anything can begin.

I have arrived,
Here,
Now.

Without presence
Action becomes empty,
And the creative impulse dead.

Witness.

Dare go in,
A bit further,
A bit deeper.

Expand,
A bit higher,
A bit wider.

Believe.

Take up the space
You deserve.

Deep gratitude
Only knows
The NOW.

Yet it remembers.

Real danger

Lies

In silencing

What needs

To be witnessed.

All paths of comparison
Are dead ends.

And often worse than that.

They are the gun
You hold up
To your own temple.

I have nothing
To give
If I abandon
My well,
And forget
My way
Back to source.

Betraying myself
For the sake of others
Will only bring
Pain and resentment.

The heavy load
People will try
And dump onto you,

The repeated stories
And patterns
They will want to
Involve you in,

The blame and shame
They will generously offer,

Are neither your cross
To bare,
Nor your burden
To carry.

Love yourself enough
To set healthy boundaries,
To lend a helping hand.

But do not take on

What isn't yours
To lift,
Hold,
And carry.

2/2

There is no place big enough
To hide your greatness.

So why carry on trying.

Your Divine self
Relies on your Earthly existence
To share
What it has to share.

Don't let it down.

When we do not seek

With every inch of our being

To sharpen

And elevate

Our awareness,

We are at risk

Of falling

Into the traps

Of flattery,

Distortion,

And delusion.

We basically become

A prey

To our own sleepwalking.

I am completely ordinary.

Just like you are you,
I am me.

That is the most extra-ordinary
We can be.

Sometimes we need
To be reminded
To fiercely prioritise
Love over fear.

Be a rebel.

Choose intuition
Over one-sided information.

Choose your inner compass
Rather than random directions.

Choose to rest,
And not give up.

Plant those seeds
Dear one,
Even if it seems in vain.

Before you know it
They will have grown
Into trees.

Unless of course,
You've planted
Runner beans or strawberries.
Then you will most likely get
Runner beans or strawberries!

Which to be fair,
Sounds quite good to me.

Be in love
With who you are,
With all that you are.

Do not look at yourself
Through distorted filters.

Do not see yourself
With the eyes of shame,

But rather with the compassion
You have worked so hard
To grow in your beautiful heart.

Systems and modalities
Are only helpful
Up to a point.

If you let them
Clip your wings
And put you in a cage,
Then you have forgotten
Your true essence and potential.

By all means,
Learn from the systems and modalities.

But do not fall asleep.
Do not follow blindly.

Stay awake and curious.

Your life is so much more
Than what you are
Often led
To believe.

Give your wings

Space and opportunities

To grow,

And soar.

Refuse to live a lie.

Use the inner compass
You were born with.

Your body is a temple of infinite wisdom,
That carries the universe
And its laws within itself.

Its practical, emotional,
And spiritual intelligence
Is far greater
Than any elaborate scientific discovery
Humankind has ever made.

Its direct access to source
Makes it an uncanny and trustworthy ally.

Listen to it.

Be an example.
Show the way
To true bridging and collaboration
Across fields.

# Wild, Authentic, and Perfectly Imperfect

Be loud
Be silent
Be bleak
Be colourful

Be YOU.

The sharpness of the thorns
Has never scared me.

I am more intimidated
By the beauty and scent
Of the rose itself.

I wear my scars

With pride

For they are a testimony

Of the many generations

Of wounds

That have now healed.

I am not scared of the wound.
I am not scared of the scar.
I am not scared of the sun
Lighting the moon from afar.

I am not scared of the cracks.
I am not scared of the light.
I am not scared of the darkness
Delighting me with such insight.

I am not scared of the wound.
I am not scared of the scar.
I am not scared of the sun
Lighting the moon from afar.

Some days, she is that fragile rose petal.
Other days, those strong tree roots.

Some days, she is the dancing leaves.
Other days, the growing branches.

Some days, she is the bud about to blossom.
Other days, the thorn guarding the castle.

But please, always treat her with kindness.

For you may not know
On that particular day,
Whether she is
Laughing inside,
Holding a sword,
Or filled with tears
Too heavy to cry.

Perfection
Is the biggest lie
And distortion
Of all.

There is no need
To thrive to be unique.

You ARE unique
And there is NOTHING
You can do about it!

Allow yourself to be
BIG
And BOLD.

Allow yourself to be
SOFT
And GENTLE.

Allow yourself
To embrace,
Embody,
And be seen
As the unique,
And beautiful
Expression
Of YOU
That you are.

My vulnerability
Is my strength.

My openness,
My courage.

The time has come
To speak up.

I have the deepest GRATITUDE
For my unconventional
Priorities.

There is absolutely no need
To bend to the extent of cracking.

There is no extra grace
In uprooting and exposing yourself
To the violent winds of their dismissal.

Breathe deep my love,
And stay rooted in your integrity.
Stand as tall as the tree that you are.

You do not have to shrink, ever.

When the pain becomes unbearable,
Allow it to flow through you.

Know that this pain too will pass
As the tears stream down your trunk,
Cleanse your bark,
And water your roots.

When the exposure 1/2

To the elements is too much,
Shelter in the embrace of the Divine,
Rest in the arms of Mama Earth,
Receive the unconditional love
And gifts you so deserve.

You are of the Earth.
You are of the Stars.

You are safe.

And you are loved.

2/2

Show up
For what brings you
Joy,
And makes you feel
Alive.

I am excited
About this 'being alive' thing!

I can no longer afford
To fight against myself,
To fight against my differences.

I do not want to anymore.

It is time for me
To reclaim my uniqueness,
To own it,
And celebrate it - fully.

No more shrinking
No more hiding
No more bleaching.

No more shame.

From now on,
I am me 1/2

And will reveal

What needs to be revealed.

Feel,

Sense,

Move,

Like a wolf,

And your path will become clear.

My job

Is to show up every day

In whatever way

Feels authentic.

To learn the art

Of detachment.

To become

A bit more

Like the moon.

At peace

With the cycles

And phases of life.

For she is as comfortable

Being invisible,

Forgotten,

Even ignored,

As she is,

Filling the whole sky             1/2

With such light

And power

That no one

Can miss seeing her.

2/2

I value

The gift of my life enough

To not want to

Trade it in

For someone else's

Path.

It is OK to have a bit of a 'nothing' day.

A lot goes on inside
That is constantly
And consistently
Reshaping
The universe.

Soften.

Soften my love,
Even when it feels easier to harden.

This is a challenge worth taking on.

Soften in the places
That feel unavailable
And risky.

Soften and trust.

Others may fail to see your worth.

This does not matter,
I can assure you.

What matters
Is that even in the depth of darkness,
You manage to say,

'Dear heart,
Dear body,
Dear mind,
Dear soul,
I LOVE you,
I love you UNCONDITIONALLY,
No matter who, no matter what.'

## HOW ELSE CAN I TELL YOU?

How else can I tell you
That you are Beautiful,
That you are Divine,
That you are Sacred,
That you are Worthy.

How else can I tell you
That you are a Miracle,
That you Belong,
And are Deserving of
Love and Blessings.

How else can I tell you
That you are Wonderful,
Amazing,
And Awesome
Just the way you are.

How else can I tell you
That YOU

1/3

Matter,
That YOU
Have your place
In this world.

How else can I tell you
That you are Pure Magic,
That your magic
Is like no one else's.

How else can I tell you
That you are an Irreplaceable Colour
In the stunning rainbow
That displays itself in front of your eyes.

How else can I tell you
That the world needs YOU
The way you are,
Just the way you are.

How can I tell you
That I love you

2/3

If I do not love and honour
The miracle that I am,
If I do not lead by example.

So here I stand,
Naked,
In unconditional love
For the life
That has been given to me,
For the life
That has been given to you.

Laugh.

Laugh sweet soul
Until your heart
Cracks open.

Cry.

Cry sweet soul
Until your heart
Cracks open.

There is no place
More sacred
Than the rift
Of a loving heart.

Melt into softness

And the whole universe

Will reveal itself

To you.

Sometimes you need
To go more inward
In order to break
The walls around you.

Gather

Your soul fragments

And recreate

The stunning mosaic

That is you.

I owe my tears
So much.

For they
Let me know
What I am really feeling.

By following their guidance,
I peel off
Layer after layer
Of leftover grief, anger, and pain,

Leaving room
For seeds to be planted
And a beautiful garden
To grow and blossom.

What hurts
Is only part
Of the story.

And still,

Your pain
Is valid.

How can we accompany

Our own transitions

With even more love, ease,

And tenderness

Is an essential question.

I am showing up,
Fierce and graceful.

I have learned this
From the Earth herself.

How profoundly amazing it is
That she shares her life,
With such unconditional love,
Generosity, and warmth.

I've started
Doing ME
And it's deliciously
Contagious.

When you keep censoring

Parts of who you are,

You literally stab yourself

In the back,

And heart,

Over and over again,

Leaving yourself

Bleeding

On the side of the road.

# **COMMITMENT AND DEVOTION**

Choose

*

Let Go

*

Reclaim

Today
I take responsibility
For my life.

I choose
To feel alive.

I choose
To show up.

# Choose

You are the only one
Who can take care
Of yourself
On a daily basis.

May your steps be aligned
With your body,
Your body
With your heart,
Your heart
With your soul,
Your soul
With your spirit.

If you lose direction,
If you fall,
Do not judge yourself,
Do not despair.

Allow,
And welcome
Help.

1/2

Take my hand
And breathe
Into your heart.

You have all it takes
To walk, pray, connect
To that cleansing ocean,
To that nourishing well,
To that soothing river,
To that purifying fire,
To that strengthening mountain.

I am ALWAYS
By your side,
Cheering you on.

Remember
To look with new eyes,
To listen with open ears,
And to observe with a sense of wonder.

Keep rediscovering yourself,
Your surroundings, the landscape, and others,
Every day, minute, second.

This is essential practise.
Do not undervalue it.
Do not become blasé.

Rest.
But don't EVER settle
For a drop of laziness
In your curiosity,
Or even an inch of stagnation
In your enthusiasm.

For these are vampires, life thieves
That can dampen

The most innocent and joyful heart.

Be patient.
But know when to stop waiting around.

Be curious and adventurous,
In small and big ways.

Be passionate,
And take passion to its highest level,
With integrity and respect.

Honour yourself, life, and all that is.

Only then,
Will you begin to notice
Your sparkly wings.

2/2

Today I will focus
On loving myself.

On loving my light,
On loving my darkness,
On loving my blossoms,
On loving my wounds.

On loving ALL of me.

It is NOT my job
To control the outcome.

But it is my job to keep
Shaping,
And reshaping
My vision.

I am building
A cathedral.

Not with the stones of others,
Not with the aim to impress.

But with the intangible knowing
That this cathedral
Needs to be built.

The portal has opened.

The job of an undercover warrior of peace
Is to recommit to this path
On a daily basis.

The work is never finished.
There is always
More peace, more love
To strive for, and welcome.

Hope is beautiful.

The door slowly shuts again.

I am a bit further
On my path
Than I was a moment ago.

Once you start
Showing up
For yourself,
You no longer seek
The approval
And praise of others.

You never again
Wait for someone else's permission
To FULLY live
And honour
Your own life.

You are here
To heal
The universal wound
By simply embracing
ALL that you are.

There is nothing wrong
With you.

It is the relationship
With yourself
That needs extra love,
Care, and tenderness.

And remember
To not take yourself
So seriously.

Look in the mirror,
Laugh at, and with, yourself.

When you manage to allow humour
Into your daily life,
Your heart starts to smile again.

It is vital
To take
Individual responsibility
For our life.

To develop discipline.
To renew the commitment
To our calling.

To rest when needed.

To listen
To what truly matters.
To hear it.

To honour it
By taking the next
Inspired step.

When we do not show up
For ourselves,
The universe struggles
To find ways
To help and support us.

I take responsibility

For my incarnation,

For the cleansing of my energy,

For the integrity of my intention and offerings,

For the lion's courage of my heart.

I renew my commitment

To be of service,

And to persevere,

Even when I want to give up.

All this,

While listening

To my own sacred flow and rhythm.

I will hold space for your emotions.

But I will neither entertain nor feed
The thoughts that disempower you
And pull you back into drama,
Leading you to live a life
On the back row,
While the Shakespearean tragedy
Is stuck on repeat,
Depriving you
Of the simple, yet precious
Gift of today.

Instead, I will hold a mirror in front of you,
And pray you see yourself,
Your story, and your life,
From a different angle,
From a higher perspective,
From a renewed sense of love and presence.

If you are unhappy
With your life,
Make one small change.

Whether it be
In attitude or action.

This will go a long way.

Nothing will shift
Unless you infuse
New life into it.

When you decide
To call parts of your soul back,
Vow to not abuse them,
To not abandon them.

Create a life
In which they can relax
And blossom.

I choose
To have my own back.

To invite myself
Into the arena.

To cheer MYSELF on.

This is TRUE self-love
And embodied empowerment.

Drop the masks,
Don't be scared.

Break the chains,
Don't de frightened.

Push back the limits,
Don't be afraid.

And if you are
Scared, frightened, and afraid,
Do it anyway.

You carry the magic,
Guidance, and support
Of the universe
Inside you.

If you doubt yourself enough,
You will believe
Your doubts.

If you believe in yourself enough,
You will believe
In yourself.

The choice is yours.

Do not underestimate
How powerful you are.

Choose
How you use
Your thoughts and energy,
Wisely.

Be grateful.
Grateful for this moment,
For the warmth seeping through
The panels of the window,
For the light making its way
Through the cracks of your being.

Be grateful.
Grateful for your wounds,
As they are living reminders
Of how much you can love,
Of how much you have lived and survived.

Be grateful.
Grateful for your story,
As it carves out your unique path
In the depth of this forest called life,
As it paints a rainbow
Never to be seen elsewhere.

Be grateful.
Grateful for the awareness

That you are not your story,
But that she is
The blossoms and leaves
On your tree.

Be grateful.
Grateful for your soaring heart
And strong pulse,
For the ever flowing rivers,
And the intricate mandalas,
Living inside you.

2/2

Every now and then
I need to remind myself

That I am not
Part of the consciousness police,
And do not aspire to belong
To the moralist club,

Even though,
I do have strong values!

I choose

To allow myself

To trust,

And receive.

I remember that moment
When time stopped.

'Hope is what's left
When everything else is gone.
It's a pathetic illusion.
It means there is
Nothing worthwhile
Still possible.'
He said.

I was so shocked.

I had to think about it,
For a while.

To say I was completely puzzled
Is an understatement.
It was like receiving
A dagger right in the heart.
Like witnessing
The earthquake

1/3

Of my entire belief system.

'Perhaps this is true.
Perhaps he is right.'
I thought to myself.
He did state this
With such authority and conviction.

'What IS hope after all?'
I wondered…

After some time
And consideration
I decided to consciously choose
Hope over cynicism,
Love over hate.

I chose to believe
In miracles over resignation,
In magic over dullness.

These simple choices

Have filled my life
With so much more fun and joy.

And so it is.

Hope is real,
If we allow it to be.

The choice is ours.

Do not chase
From a place
Of lack.

Offer
From a place
Of abundance.

Everything changed
When I started
Having my own back.

I chose to be
In service to life herself.

What an uncanny gift
This turns out to be for me.

I choose
To define success
By the amount
Of courage,
Love,
Devotion,
Grace,
And surrender
I am able to embody.

I choose
To define success
By the way
I learn to not shame myself
When harmony
Is out of balance,
And I am needing
To embrace the shadow,
Before I can return to the light.

Can you promise
Your heart
That you have your own back,
No matter what?

Having your own back
Is the greatest gift
You can give yourself.

If this seems like a super weird concept,
Start practising it today.

I can assure you
That your life
Will change
For the better.

Remember
That you don't need
Anyone else
To give you permission
To be yourself.

Only you,
Can truly do that.

I choose
To remember
To never live my life
Walking on eggshells.

There is no need to shrink
In order to be kind.

I choose innocence
And playfulness
To guide me
Through today.

And I choose
To receive,
As generously
As I give.

# Let Go

I am learning
To let go
Of expectations
Without losing sight
Of my vision.

Whoosh,
What a ride.

We often try
And measure our worth
Against what other people
Think of us,
And how they treat us.

But our worth
Has absolutely
Nothing to do
With what we seemingly
Achieve
Or don't achieve.

Let alone
Having anything to do
With anyone else.

I should have known
You felt threatened
By my power and aliveness
When you mistook
My belly laugh
And ecstatic joy
For a wish
To take
Something away from you.

Still, years have passed,
And the echo
Of my laughter
Carries on,
Untamed.

Do not seek
Recognition
Or applause.

Simply allow
Yourself
To be seen,
To be witnessed.

Welcome
And receive
The acknowledgement,
The praise,
If they come your way.

I can assure you
That this choice will be
Your greatest victory.

How liberating it is
To reach a phase of life
Where there is
Neither a need
For approval,
Nor a wish
To hide.

May I give
The job of evaluating
The worth of my offerings
To the gods,
The stars,
The planets,
The universe.
And even, to my cat.

But dear Lord,
Not to myself!

To let go

Of all expectations

While remaining open

Frees the heart and soul.

Let go
Of the need
To have an impact,
And surrender
To the truth itself.

You ARE positively
Impactful,
Just by being you.

I release
My impatience with others,
My frustration and triggers,
By simply taking action
When I need to take action.

Those feelings and triggers
Are usually not
About anyone else, really.
They are about self.

Let's start dismantling
Judgement, blame, and shame.

People do their best
With what they have access to,
Within themselves,
In that unique moment in time.

That does not mean
You should put up
With disrespectful behaviour.

But what it does mean,
Is that you do not need to lose energy,
Either holding on to their story,
Taking on the role of the moral police,
Or even trying to fix their life.

This is not your job.

As you know too well,
The mind loves
To trick us
In believing
All sorts of random lies.

Well, I'd say it's our duty
To let go of assuming
It knows best,
And develop a few skills
To get our own back.
Maybe even trick it, ourselves,
By unapologetically following
Our heart and intuition.

Don't you agree?

Once you have done
All you can,
Surrender
To the bigger plan.

I let go
Of the fear of disturbing
By unapologetically
Being who I am.

I let go of the fear
Of falling off the pedestal
I never asked to,
Nor wanted to,
Be put on.

What a relief
This all is.

And...
I love being myself,
Fully rooted,
With my feet firmly on the ground.

# Reclaim

You owe it to yourself
To step up
And reclaim
Your power,
Your sword.

You are a warrior
Of peace,
Of beauty,
Of mystic union,
With all that is.

You're not the piece of shit
You think you are,
Or even worse,
Believe you are.

You are PURE magic.

Discussion closed.

Here I stand
In awe and gratitude,
Celebrating
ALL that I am,
Celebrating
ALL that you are.

Do you believe me now?

Do you believe me now
When I tell you
How Beautiful, Divine, and Sacred
YOU are, just the way you are.

Do you believe me now
When I tell you
How Perfect you are,
Just the way you are.

Reclaim your power.
Call back your tribe.
Invite your muse.

Write yourself back to life,
Dance yourself back to life,
Paint yourself back to life,
Sing yourself back to life,
Cook yourself back to life,
Garden yourself back to life,
Walk yourself back to life.

Whatever your flame
Requires and dictates,
Listen dear one.

For there is nothing more worthwhile
Than to honour that flame,
Than to catch that wave of grace.

You are ready.

1/2

Ready to tend to
Your inner fire.

Ready to catch
That wave of grace.

My work
Is not a business.

It is a way of life.

I am constantly reminded

That the agony

Of hiding parts of myself

Is far greater

Than the growing pains

Of allowing myself

To be fully seen.

I absolutely
LOVE
Being silent.

So I honour this,
When I plan my day.

What do you absolutely LOVE being, doing?
Identify it,
So you can make sure
You honour it each day.

No one deserves
The burden
Of the pedestal.

No one deserves
To be adulated,
And then pushed off,
Mocked, ridiculed,
By jealous and hungry crowds.

No.

No one deserves
To be put on a pedestal.

From today onwards
I retrieve,
Reclaim,
Honour,
Celebrate,

ALL that I am.

The wonders and delight,
The darkness and light,
The mystery and predictability,
The chaos and clarity,

All woven in the deserts and oceans,
And filled with the nectar of 'to be'.

I am fiercely
Independent
- with a twist.

I am in awe

Of the person
I am becoming,

Of the person
I always was.

All creations
Are multidimensional.

Me included.

You included.

Isn't it marvellous?

Repeat after me:

I am a magnet for
Abundance,
Miracles,
And ease.

And so it is.

Reclaim
Your voice
And the courage
To use it.

Do it now.

There is no more time
To lose.

Welcome validation, praise
With an open heart
And gratitude.

But don't fall through the trap
Of waiting for these to happen
In order to give you
False permission to create
Whatever the hell you want to create.

Simply reclaim
YOUR right
To do so.

And do it!

Your creative fire
Longs for this.

Yes I am a witch.

I listen to the inner voice
That whispers guidance and wisdom,
And I share it.

I will not be silenced.
I will not give in to fear.

I release old memories.

This time around
I will not be burnt
Or silenced.

I choose to bring forth
The multidimensional being
That I am born to be.

I am open to the knowing
I came to this Earth with,
And choose to honour and respect it,      1/3

First and foremost.

This is not arrogance.
This is deep respect for life itself.

Yes I am a witch.

I call it
Being connected
To one's intuition,
Being tuned in,
Switched on,
Plugged it.

I call it
Living one's life
In harmony
With the infinite potential
That is given to us
As divine beings,
Incarnated in human form.

2/3

Yes I am a witch.

Not a single part of me
Will remain cast out
This time.

I speak and sing
From the darkness of the womb,
And the brightness of the stars.

Yes I am a witch,
And proud to be.

# **DEDICATION AND CO-CREATION**

The Return of the Muse, Patience,
and Perseverance

*

Soul Activation

*

Co-Creation with Source

How can I embrace
A path of unconditional
Devotion,
Commitment,
And soul-led living?

How can I not...

# The Return of the Muse, Patience, and Perseverance

Call your muse back.

NOW.

LOUDER.

She is waiting.

We convince ourselves

That we are 'too something',

'Not enough something',

That we have missed the boat.

But really, have we?

And if by some strange circumstance or fate

We have,

There will be another boat.

There always is.

While we get caught

In our delusional and distorted beliefs,

Our muse falls asleep,

Visits someone else,

Self-destroys,

Gets bored.

And yet, she never

Truly goes away,

And never, ever gives up on us.

1/2

She always hears
The slightest whisper
From our soul,
The softest cry
From our heart.

She is like a mother
Who can sense
Her baby has woken up
Before she even hears a sound.

She is always there
Reminding us
That our boat
Is our breath,
Our heartbeat,
Our creative impulse,
Our inner light,
And flame.

She is always there,
Ready to answer our call. 2/2

If there's one thing
I cannot do,
It is to play Russian roulette
With my creativity.

It is rude
To shut the door
In the face of inspiration.

Just think for a moment.

Would you do that
To an innocent guest
Bringing you
A bunch of colourful, scented flowers?

The sacred garden
Of my destiny
Is bursting
With perfume, colours,
Textures, and sounds.

There is a glimpse of you
In every raindrop,
In every blossom,
In every seed,
In every breeze.

There is a feeling of you
With every step,
With every glance,
With every embrace.

There is you,
In all that is,
And all that will ever be.

You are that mysterious sparkle,           1/2

That mystical echo,
Walking me home,
Each day.

How would you welcome
A vulnerable friend
Eager to share
Their deepest dreams and visions?

I thought so….

Remember this
When your soul
Knocks at the door of your heart,
And your muse
Invites you to dance.

It is hugely dangerous,
And disrespectful
To ignore them both.

Howl
Howl
Howl

From the depths of your being,

And the door will open.

I write songs to process life
And weave more beauty.

I am taking the risk,
To show up,
To live,
To feel,
To build,
To share,
To love,
To be seen,
To be heard,
To be loved,
To be rejected,
To be abandoned,
To be forgotten.

I am taking the risk.
Meet me there.

Perhaps I am finally
Getting in touch
With my visions.

The last few years
I have reconnected
To my voice,
To my sound,
To the medicine music
That lives inside me.

What an exquisite gift
I have been given.

But there could be
No bypassing,
No shortcuts.

I had to die
To be reborn.

Now my muse,
Spirit, and soul
Rejoice,
Dance,
Celebrate,

Using my body
As their sacred temple and theatre.

My multidimensional being
Welcomes this divine and timely expansion.

And the song bearer
Awaits to give birth
On this Earth,
Once more.

2/2

Just in case
You are wondering
Or had forgotten.

Your muse
Will NEVER
Give up
On you.

While I am learning
To trust myself again,

May I forgive,
Comfort,
And love myself,
Unconditionally.

My calling
Is unfolding
In front of my own eyes.

Long has it awaited,
With trapped wings
Inside my heart,
For me
To be ready.

To carry
The creative impulse
Through,
Is one of the most
Undervalued skills
And blessings.

I have come to realise
With such uncanny clarity
That writing songs
Is one of the main ways
For me to acknowledge and integrate
Events, feelings, thoughts, emotions, and stories.

So yes it can feel
Uncomfortable to share.

It is like being cut open on the operation table
With no anaesthetic,
And being left there indefinitely
As people walk by.

With some songs,
The whole process
Has been completed,
The sewing up performed.
With others,
The journey is ongoing.

1/2

I often ask myself
If there is actually a purpose
In sharing them.

And then my heart screams
As loud as it can
That of course there is,
That I must show up
In whatever way
Honours the alchemist of life
That I am.

To learn to hold
The thought, the wish, the idea, the dream
Without smothering them
Requires presence, focus, and practice.

To allow them to flow
To their final destination
And blossom,
Demands patience, trust, craftsmanship
And most of all,
Consistent dedication.

Stay focused
My love.

Stay focused.

We are all here,
Cheering you on.

You are doing just fine.

Deep commitment
Ripples,
And creates
The most unexpected,
Delicious patterns.

When you honour
Your commitment to self,
You experience your own reliability.
You start trusting yourself more.
And as a result, you grow in confidence.

When you let yourself down,
Again and again,
You give yourself
The 'I can't trust this person' message,
As well as a reason to stay stuck
In that destructive cycle.

Persevere with the things
You feel excited by
Despite the lack
Of external validation.

Trust me.

The golden reward
Will be far beyond
Your hopes and imagination,
Far beyond
Anything
You may have wished for.

First, you must prioritise
Presence over frantic planning
And strategising.

Only once you show up
Present and available,
Can you make inspired plans
For future power moves.

Does the cat give up

Every time

It misses a fly or a mouse?

Does the bee sulk

When the flower

It has chosen

Has little nectar?

Be the cat.

Be the bee.

Allow yourself
To feel disheartened,
Even discouraged
If that is what is coming up for you.

When the time
For choice arises,
Always choose courage,
Always choose your heart.

Do not feed discouragement
Until you end up swallowed by it,
Until you become
Discouragement itself.

Instead,
Grow your heart forces,
BECOME courage,
Embody the lion that you are.

# Soul Activation

.f

ɾe

I am the voice of my ancestors.

I am swan

I am water

I am the grace of lost lovers.

I am bear

I am mountain

I am the bones of my creators.

I am eagle

I am wind

I am the vision of my grandmothers.

I am spirit

I am earth

I am the breath of faint murmurs.

I am lion

I am roar

1/2

I am the courage of my grandfathers.

I am wolf

I am fire

I am the voice of my ancestors.

NEVER to be silenced again.

I am giving myself
Permission to shine
With the full amount
Of vitality and creativity
I have been entrusted with.

Pay attention
To your inner flame.
For without her,
You are not.

Hold space for her to emerge
From the ashes, and grow tall.

With her, you'll feel alive again.

You'll feel fear but also excitement,
You'll wish to go on adventures,
You'll have a sense of belonging.

And you'll know,
Deep inside your bones,
That this is home,
That seeking can be
Playful and fun,
Free from the burden
Of right and wrong.

1/2

Become the observer.

Tend to the embers.
Nourish the flame.

Live
With your inner fire lit.

*Evening musings*

I want to be
The very best version of myself,
Just as you are
The very best version of yourself.

I want to be as me,
As you are you.

I don't want to be you,
I just want to be me.

Just as you are you,
Just as I am me.

And yet,
Aren't you me,
And I, you?

When a woman disconnects

From her inner fire

For too long,

She becomes a magnet

To other lost souls

Who treat her

In ways that confirm to her,

Those feelings of unworthiness.

For let it be clear,

She IS lost.

Caught in past woundings,

Battling, and self-destroying

In her own death trap.

Now without boundaries,

Blindly addicted

To drama and submission,

Dry of life forces,

Joy and pleasure.

She has LITERALLY lost herself,

And desperately needs to be reminded
Of her uncanny power, beauty, and courage.

So when you meet a woman
Who has disconnected
From her inner fire,
Do not judge her,
Do not pity her.

Fan your flames with all you have
So that your fire may burn stronger,
And light her way back home.

Home, to her embers,
Home, to her fire,
Home, to her precious inner compass.

We question

Our right to exist

As if we were on trial,

Constantly on alert.

Checking

Whether we are worthy enough

To be here.

This must end.

This must end NOW.

We are not on trial.

Life HAS been given to us to live.

Perhaps we have a soul contract,

Perhaps not...

But there is no fine print,

Neither on the card

Nor at the bottom of the contract.

The weavings
Of our lives,
Destinies,
And connections
Are made of
Unbreakable threads.

I celebrate myself

For showing up,
For committing,
For persevering,
For dedicating my life
To this quest and path.

I am not sure why,
But this feels like
One of the most moving
And extraordinary things
I have ever done for myself.

I will no longer silence
The cries of my soul.

I will no longer darken
The eager bright paints
At the tip of my fingers and toes,
Ready to colour
The paths, the journeys, the roads.

Long have I waited,
Not with remorse,
Discouragement or impatience,
Not with blindness or delusion,
But with faith and trepidation.

And longer still
Have I waited
With the dance
Of the universe
Inside my body,
Knowing that soon
It will be time.                               1/2

Time to break free
From the imaginary chains.

Time to sing the song
Of the entire universe.

Time to pull down the distorted veils
With my feet deeply anchored on Mother Earth.

Time to dance and colour the paths,
The journeys,
The roads.

And YES,
The time IS NOW.

I will never again

Turn down the volume

And brightness

Of my passion

And enthusiasm

To make you feel safe.

Commit to yourself
With the depth of faithfulness
You would want someone else
To commit to you.

We must show up,

First and foremost,

Embodying who we truly are,

As a sign of respect

And gratitude

For the life

That has been gifted to us,

So generously.

Let the ripples
Of your human heart
Dance to the beat, rhythm,
And crackling of fire.

Rebuild the sacred circle of creation,
Where nothing is shamed,
And all is to be discovered.

Then, let's meet,
In that sacred circle,
Where the ripples
Of our human hearts
Dance freely to the beat, rhythm,
And crackling of fire.

Rise
Dear soul,
Rise

From the depths of eternity.

Dance
Dear soul,
Dance

For the human spirit
Is still strong.

May I offer

Nothing less

Than the nectar

That has been given to me,

Than the nectar

That has given ITSELF to me.

I can no longer
Think or understand.

So let me enter
The realm of dream
And mystic dance.

Only there,
Can I find solace
And peace.

I invite you
To allow
And welcome
Your soul
To fully
Anchor itself
In your sacred temple,
Your body.

I will never say this enough.

We are not prisoners.
We are co-creators
Of our reality.

Truly.

Gathering soul fragments
And releasing them deep into the earth.

Gathering soul fragments
And blowing them high into the stars.

Gathering soul fragments
And becoming whole,
Becoming one,
With all of creation,

Once again.

# Co-Creation with Source

Have you ever thought

That perhaps life's deepest wish

Is to co-create with you?

Thank you universe
For your guidance,
Teachings,
And healing,
Always.

No other star
Can make
Your star
Shine brighter.

No other star
Can dim
Your light either.

You are given
All you need
For your radiance.

Look around.

Notice
How wonderful
It is to shine
Amongst billions
Of other stars,
How ecstatic
It feels to melt

Into the milky way,
And become
The bearer and messenger
Of this uncanny magic.

This,
Dear one,
Is true belonging.

I think
I might have become the ocean.

So many waves
Growing and crashing,
Inside and around me.

Yet, peace prevails.

Oh glorious sun
Of a thousand echoes,

May your light
Bless me on my path.
May your warmth
Soften my heart.
May your radiance
Help my being expand
To the sacred sanctuary
Of infinite galaxies.

So that it too,
May radiate
Its unborn gifts.

The veil between worlds
Is getting thinner.

This makes me happy.

You cannot expect
Friends to like
What you create.

You cannot expect
Family to like
What you create.

You cannot expect
Strangers to like
What you create.

But know that
When you create with integrity,
When you create from the heart,

The whole universe
Celebrates you,
Supports you,
Embraces you,
And cheers you on.

The spirits dance
With, and for us.

We are the spirits,
They are us.

I cannot remember
The day I decided
To leave it all behind
To come to Earth.

But that was a BIG day.

That was a BIG decision.

Yet my soul has not forgotten.

She reminds me regularly
That I haven't left
Anything behind.

On the contrary,
I have brought it all with me,
To share.

Come back to source.

Come back to the intimate dance
Between in and out,
Between wild and peaceful,
Between ecstasy and nothingness.

I am sitting
By the river.

Alone,
And yet, not alone.

Join me,
If you too
Dare
To listen
To the mystery
Of the flowing water.

I hug Grandfather Tree,
For his strength
And wisdom
Call me.

My sap is his sap.
I am no different from him.
He is my mirror.
I am his echo.

I sit by Sister River,
For her everlasting flow
And gentle song
Call me.

My murmur is her murmur.
I am no different from her.
She is my mirror.
I am her echo.

I lie on Mother Earth,
For her comfort,

Grounding, and nourishing
Call me.

My heartbeat is her heartbeat.
I am no different from her.
She is my mirror.
I am her echo.

Spirit loves
To co-create with us.

When we allow it,
When we engage with it,
Is when magic
Truly happens.

Riding the waves.
Weaving the scarves and scores
Made of old traditions,
New energies, and divine creations.

Remembering.
Inviting new visions in.

Nothing has changed
And yet, nothing ever
Remains the same.

Still, there is much ancient wisdom
To remember and bring back into our lives
As the yearning and longing
For all that the Earth offers
Becomes stronger,
As the reaching out
To other realms
Intrigues and fascinates again,
As the dance
Between spiritual arrogance

And integrity of heart
Plays out.

There is much to learn and unlearn.

May we drop into genuine humility,
And ride these waves
With more respect, awareness,
And devotion.

I am never closer
To God
Than when I am devoted
To the process of creating.

Or is it
That I am never
More aware
Of our connection
Than when I am creating?

Either way,
I never feel more alive,
And more at home
Than when I am creating.

If we were able

To truly listen to,

And understand

The intricate songs of birds,

We would most certainly

Have the answers

To most questions

That matter.

The streams,

They sing, and sing, and sing to me,

Until I find my way,

Back to source.

Do not wait
To be given permission
To show up.

When you do show up,
Do not seek approval.

Simply drop
Into your heart.

Reestablish
Your connection to spirit.

Enter
The ecstasy
Of this present moment.

Sometimes you need
To put the question
Out there, in the universe,
Not to stop you on your tracks
As you wait for an answer,
But to light
The path ahead.

# BLISS

The Power of
Alchemy and Transmutation

*

Surrendering to a Blissful Life

Welcome bliss
Into your life,
And it will bless you
With more and more
Deliciousness
Each day.

# The Power of Alchemy and Transmutation

Blessed be

The connections

That help us grow.

I will be fine
Without you.

The whole universe
Has embraced me.

Betrayal comes with a hidden gift
Wrapped inside its womb.

The gift of becoming so fierce
In one's honouring of self
That nothing can deter us from this task,
And most importantly,
Never will we abandon, reject, or betray
Our own heart and soul again.

This gift is perhaps
The biggest opportunity
We will ever be given in this lifetime.

Once we have begun
The grieving and healing process,
It is up to us
To take this opportunity
Or to leave it behind.

Some days
The most honest thing
You can do,
Is simply to feel the disappointment.

From that soft, vulnerable place,
You will know
What really matters to you.

You can then begin to engage
In rebellious hope,
Until you are able to
Reconnect with faith once more.

Today I had the choice
To give up
Or to keep seeing life
As the mysterious miracle
That she is,
Unfolding
Before my eyes.

Guess which choice I made?

What about you?
Which one will you make?

Sometimes,
No matter
How much heart
You put into something,
It will not be received
In the way it was sent out.

It will not be welcomed
With the love it was created.

Feel the pain
Of this mismatch in energy.

But don't give up
On your beautiful heart,
Dreams, and creations.

We seek refuge and safety
In the most peculiar places.

Smile at this.

Laugh at yourself.

Laugh WITH yourself.

Distorted perception is certainly
A very common staple diet
Amongst us humans!

The cycle of life
Moves through the seasons,
Fragile yet unstoppable.

A sacred dance
Of death, rebirth and expansion.

A beginning, an end, a spiral.

Downwards, upwards,
Inwards, outwards.

Transforming,
Alchemizing,
And vibrating once again,
To the highest frequency available.

Notice that every hint

Of envy and jealousy

Is a distorted expression

Of your soul

Calling you home,

And needing

YOU

To fully show up

For what you have signed up to do,

Here on this beautiful planet.

I am a work
In progress.

And so are you!

Let's make sure we welcome
A bit of magic in the unfolding.

Whenever there is fear,
Excitement is near.

Choose to follow
The joyful energy of excitement.

Make excitement the driver.
Fear can ride in the back seat.

For if you give fear the wheel,
Despite its best protective intentions,
It will take the shortcut
That leads to a dead end,
Or even worse to the edge of a cliff.

And frankly,
You do not want that.

Life is short,
And yet,
Eternal.

Hard,
And yet,
So sweet.

Embrace it,
As much as you can.

Most concepts
Such as efficiency,
Achievement,
Manifestation,
Abundance,
Or even creation,
Have little to do with skill, talent, luck,
And everything to do with
Getting into gear.

First,
Notice which gear
You are in.

Is this the right gear
For that job?
For that specific moment?
For where your energy is at on that day?

Does it sound smooth?
Does it feel right?

1/2

Is your engine overworking?
Is your car shaking?

You do know how it feels
When you are
In the right gear.

So trust yourself.

Change gear if needed,
And enjoy the ride.

Prioritise re-establishing
The fundamental relationship
With, and within yourself.

As you begin that process
You will also start thriving
In more harmonious and magical
Relationships with others.

Perfection
Is obviously
An illusion
We have too long entertained.

We can put an end to this.

Firstly, by recognising
How limiting and handicapping
This concept is.

Secondly, by choosing
To see this wonky man-made disease
For what it is,
And nothing more.

You don't have to try and be perfect.
I don't have to try and be perfect.

Nothing has to,
Nor can be,
Perfect.

Everyone and everything
Is always
An ever-changing
Work in progress.

Celebrate the mess,
And the delight
That you are.

Somehow,
No matter how young
Or old we are,
We are all fresh shoots
Coming out of the mud.

If we could only
Remember
To treat this lifetime
As the precious holiday
That it is,
We would surely
Stop wasting it
In futile worries,
And would instead
Embrace each moment
With the sense of awe,
Wonder, and curiosity
It deserves.

I push the door
Open.

Fear
Turns into excitement.

I bet you know
The door I am talking about.

Have you used it recently?

To raise the vibration
Of our presence,
To hold space
For oneself,
And someone else,
Is one of the most precious gifts
We can offer in this lifetime.

For presence dissipates overwhelm.
That very overwhelm
That puts us
In freeze and panic mode.

Try dropping into full presence.
And watch alchemy at work.

Magic WILL certainly unfold.

Dear one,

You are worthy
Of your dreams,
Of your life,
Of the deepest love.

Drop the false, distorted beliefs
That make you want to hide.
They are not yours.
They do not serve you.

Trust that you can enter
This new day,
With ease and flow.

It does not have to be hard.
It does not have to be a struggle.

Embrace
That spark within you,
However buried it may be.

1/2

Have faith and dig deep.

Notice the sparkles dance
Inside and around you.

You are a high vibrational being,
Filled with light and colours,
However much darkness you experience.

Remember this.
Believe it.

Eventually,
Life will reflect
Your own sun
And moonlight
Back to you.

I am healing.
I am healed.

Both of these
Are true.

I have crossed
The paths
Of many troubled souls.

They have always,
And inadvertently
Guided me home.

The wound is the wound.
The story, the story.

The shift is now.
Available.
Arising in the present.

Freedom soars
Amongst these simple truths.

It is the quality of energy
You put into the things you do
That makes all the difference.

What kind of energy
Are you fuelling your actions with?

As the wings
Of adventure
Replace
The safety armour
Previously worn,

Excitement
Slowly transcends
Fear,
On the journey
To the unknown.

Cosmic sounds
Resonate and vibrate
In the midst of silence.

I will meet you
In that sacred space,

In the light and depth
Of your being,

In the light and depth
Of my being,

In the light and depth
Of our meeting.

At the centre of the garden,
The fire grows,
The fire roars.

I take a step forward,
Make the effort
To show up
And renew
My vows,
My genuine intention,
And dedication
To this journey called life.

Suddenly I am struck
By the same energy
That entered
The skin of the drum earlier.

I become more alive and certain
That there is
A bit of you in me,
A bit of me in you,

A bit of you
In everything,
A bit of me
In everything.

I feel a deep sense of peace,
Comfort, and gratitude.

The rain begins to fall.
It cleanses and soothes
The parts of my being
The fire could not access.

Serene, I now stand
In this Heaven upon Earth.

I carry you within me.

Such peace
Comes with this realisation.

I close my eyes
And allow this warm feeling
To envelop and blanket me.

The longing, the missing
Have magically transformed
Into a well of tenderness
And a strong sense of togetherness.

Tears run down my cheeks.
I feel unbelievably blessed.

Blessed to experience
Such unconditional love,
And embrace.

Blessed to feel

Every cell of my body,
Every inch of my bones,
Every layer of energy,
Infused with love.

Blessed
For this expansion
Into oneness.

Aho.

I allow myself
To die and be reborn,
Again and again.

Following,
Honouring,
And embracing
The sacred cycle of life.

May my medicine

Be potent enough

To attract the bees

That will make honey from it.

Each and every one of us
Has the power
To transform,
To alchemise
Shit into gold,
Wounds into medicine.

We were made this way.
We were given this ability.

It is that simple.

You will never know
How much your presence
Touched someone else's heart.

You actually may have saved their life.

Cultivate presence
Each day,
And the world
Will heal.

Show up just as you are.
You definitely won't be
Everyone's cup of tea.
(That's actually a good thing)
But you surely stand more of a chance
Of being happy that way
Than if you start chiseling
Parts of yourself
In order to fit in.

When you chisel, and chisel, and chisel
Because of shame,
You become a very strange shape;
And more importantly,
You end up living a lie.

No one wants to live a lie.
So transmute the urge to chisel,
And be your own cup of tea.

I am fascinated

By the sensual dance and alchemy

Of sound and silence.

# Surrendering to a Blissful Life

Dare to follow
Your wild heart.

Make yourself available
To miracles,

And smile.

Swan guided me here
With her grace.

She gave me
One of her feathers.

The one I now have
Tucked into my back.

The one that will dance there,
Freely and majestically,
Until the end of time.

You, my dear one,

You are
A love poem,
A mystic song,
A sensual dance,
An unfinished painting.

Perhaps awaiting for
The last strokes of colour,
Yet perfectly imperfect,
Just as you are.

I am
In awe
Of you,
Dear heart.

I remember the day
You bravely opened your heart
And were amazed,
And shocked
At the uncanny patterns
Amongst the scattered
Dust and rust.

'I had no idea,'
You said,
'How did you know they were there?'

And I answered,
'All hearts are unique kaleidoscopes,
All hearts get filled with tears,
All hearts suffer from drought,
All hearts get locked
As tight as a treasure trunk,
To make sure no one steals
The gems, beads, and gold
Buried inside them.

1/2

But even in the dark and damp,
Even in the dry and uninviting,
The heart keeps on
Creating those beautiful patterns.
And amongst them,
A few bits of scattered dust and rust.

And this my friend,
Is utterly beautiful.'

I am in love
With the mysterious flavours
Of my existence.

How lucky I am
To be alive.

Perhaps I belong
To the feline realm...

Meow.

I was born
Without opinions
Attached to my being.

I grew up
Acquiring a few,
Thinking they would
Make me feel less stupid,
More adequate,
And worthy.

It didn't work.

So I traded them in
For seeds of wonder,
Drops of hope,
Ripples of enchantment,
Sparkles of curiosity,
And rainbows of innocence.

This is one of the best decisions
I have ever made.

I encourage you
To try it out.

To come to a point

Of undeniable awareness

That hiding

Is more dangerous

Than showing up,

Is true liberation

And grace.

What is to live

But to gather,

Harvest,

Let go,

Surrender,

And weave

The remaining threads of self

Back into the universe?

Life is a wise cycle.

Trust it.

Your offerings may be ready

To grow tall and strong

Towards the light,

Or may need to stay

In the nook of the womb

A bit longer.

Either way,

Everything is fine,

JUST fine.                                          1/2

Life is a sacred gift
That has its own seasons.

Trust it.
Honour it.
Embrace it.

Fully showing up
In your own energy
Is all that is needed.

Be that innocent child
About to jump
Into the forbidden puddle.

Splash around,
Laugh,
Get wet.

Embody
The pure joy
Of playing, being,
And becoming one
With creation.

Look at the world
And yourself
With new eyes.

Listen
With owl's ears.

Pay attention.

In that moment
Of pure attentiveness,
You are fully alive and free.

Free from any system,
Label,
Conditioning,
And programming.

It is just you,
The puddle,
And spirit.

Can you hear
That laughter,
Your laughter,
Echoing
Far, far, far
In eternity?

2/2

May I respect life enough
To not question,
Nor doubt
The beauty and uniqueness
She has given me.

Last night I was given
A beautiful gift.

I dreamt
Of a new way
Of flying.

This morning
I finally noticed
My wings.

How magical it is

When intention

And commitment

Rise above attachment,

And leave

The whole dance floor

To surrender and grace.

Help me weave
This mystic night,
In which darkness and velvet
Answer the call
Of our beating hearts,

In which mystery
Dances wildly, and freely
Upon the earth,

Yet touches the heavens,
Before slowly melting
Into the light
Of the full moon.

I love spirals,
And their dancing energy.

Magical wheels of petals
From this luscious flower
Called life.

Forever turning.
Forever growing.

What if becoming one with life
Was just about dropping
A bit more
Into trust,
And feeling
That very trust
Fill us to the brink,
As our wings
Begin to grow?

Love the life
That you ARE.

Show up,
Following your inner guidance,
Fiercely and courageously,
Genuine, soft, and vulnerable,

Show up,
In honour of your incarnation
On this beautiful planet.

I listen.

I drop into presence.

I allow
My body to speak,
My soul to incarnate,
My heart to soar.

I invite
All the possible miracles
To dance through my being,
On their way into the world.

I am one
With this fleeting moment,
Just as I am one
With eternity.

I surrender to trust,
Again and again,

A bit more each time.

Untangling the knots,
Uncovering the layers,
Revealing the jewels.

Allow yourself
To step into
Your potential.

Be fierce,
Initiate.

Be brave,
Let go.

Be graceful,
Flow.

Be vulnerable,
Feel.

Be resourceful,
Create.

Silence weaves

The most exquisite songs

Within the tapestry

Of the forest.

Listen.

I find that

Not having to communicate

Other than through

What has been created,

Is pure bliss.

Often when I am worried,
It is gratitude
That brings me back
To peace.

I have a poetic vision
Of the world.

I am proud of that.

And I am committed
To blossoming
Within that vision.

I chose
To pay attention,
And the wonders of life
Offered themselves to me
With the abandon and curiosity
Of a lover.

I am a creative mystic
Entering the sacred dance
Of deep honouring,
Connection,
And bliss.

# Epilogue

In volume II of this series, I reminded you that You Are the Medicine. I hope and trust you are reclaiming this truth.

I'd love us to have, and show, more respect for the Earth, the Cosmos. To strive to walk with grace, balance, and care as we learn to embody our essence and enter the sacred dance of giving and receiving with love, joy, and celebration. As we invite our soul to freely shine through, remembering we can choose how to show up for this life and break the chains that keep us from shining our unique light. When we allow ourselves to shine, we do not blind others, we inspire them to shine too. We often seek to belong, forgetting we already belong. For we are weavings from the stars and Earth; tapestries from the deserts, oceans, mountains, and the Milky Way. ALL perfectly imperfect - which in itself is a wonderful thing.

My wish for you, for us, for humanity is that we start living, more aware and in deeper harmony with the elements, the cycles, and all that life teaches us each day. So that we may blossom and fly on the wings of surrender and bliss.

Whether you have journeyed with these soul activating pages from deep within the wound with volume I, or have landed directly in the arena with volume III, I thank you for taking this journey, back to you, back to source, and for committing to humbly showing up. I believe that this is the key to a more in tune, connected, and harmonious world.

These pages are filled with simple pearls of ancient, yet timeless wisdom that lie deep within each one of us and ask to be unveiled. They call us to reclaim our inner power and take inspired action as the beautiful co-creators of reality that we are.

If you have been reminded of this, and feel a little light growing inside you while reading my words, then I am happy. My work is done.

Let's sprinkle the world with extra hope, love, and magic. Let's be the rebels it needs, and is waiting for.

# Dedication

This last volume of *The Soul Letters You Never Received* is dedicated to all you brave beings who dare, in one way or another, to listen to your soul, to expand your heart, to step into the unknown, and challenge what keeps your wings clipped and your gifts trapped.

To you who chooses to embody the medicine you have come to this Earth with.

To you who chooses vulnerability, authenticity, and fierceness, over and over again

To you who is committed to transmuting fear and chooses to infuse life with more love, respect, trust, and harmony.

To you who weaves beauty, creativity, and generosity into every step you take.

And finally, to you, who each day, does your best to show up for this life, even when it feels unbearably hard and impossible. I thank you, and bow to you.

# About The Author

Natacha Dauphin is a singer-songwriter, sound channel, embodied holistic voice specialist, soul activator who believes her craft is a bridge between worlds, that the words in her books are portals and were sent as letters from her ancestors, the life around her, and spirit. Events and circumstances meant she had to grow up too quickly, but always felt guided inwardly—to strive for peace and forgiveness versus resentment and bitterness, which has allowed her to explore the artistry of her wounded journeys with comfort, spaciousness, and possibility. She feels emotional wounds are beautiful and mysterious, and hold precious keys to leading a freer, more authentic, joyful life. She also believes in miracles, creativity, the power of choice, and the human heart. She's now living her own dream by sharing her books, helping others find their voice, and embracing every minute of her time here on Earth.

www.natachadauphin.com

Have you read:

Letters From The Wound, volume 1 of
*The Soul Letters You Never Received* series?

\*

You Are the Medicine, volume 2 of
*The Soul Letters You Never Received* series?

\*\*\*

Find them on Amazon Worldwide

or

Contact me directly to get your signed copies at:
honouringyourcreativefire@gmail.com
www.natachadauphin.com

Printed in Great Britain
by Amazon